DID THE ROMANS EAT CHIPS?

And Other Questions About History

Paul Mason

Raintree
Chicago, Illinois

Edited by Dan Nunn, Rebecca Rissman,
   and John-Paul Wilkins
Designed by Steve Mead
Original illustrations © Capstone Global Library Ltd 2013
Illustration by HL Studios
Picture research by Mica Brancic
Production by Sophia Argyris
Originated by Capstone Global Library Ltd

Library of Congress Cataloging-in-Publication Data
Cataloging-in-Publication data is available at the
Library of Congress: loc.gov

ISBN 978-1-4109-5198-4 (hardback)
ISBN 978-1-4109-5204-2 (paperback)

Acknowledgments
We would like to thank the following for permission to
reproduce photographs: Alamy pp. 9 (© Ancient Art
& Architecture Collection Ltd), 15 (© Lesley Pardoe),
23 (© akg-images), 25 (© imagebroker/Rosseforp), 27
(© North Wind Picture Archives); Corbis p. 7 (© Werner
Forman); Getty Images pp. 16 (Keystone/Hulton
Archive), 19 (The Bridgeman Art Library); Imperial
War Museum p. 17 Monopoly set; iStockphoto pp. 14
Queen Elizabeth (© Steven Wynn), 14 toilet (© Rouzes);
Library of Congress p. 13 (Prints and Photographs
Division Washington, D.C. 20540 USA); Shutterstock
pp. 4 potatoes (© Nattika), 4 Roman legionary soldier
(© Nejron Photo), 4 brown bag (© Lim ChewHow),
5 pouring honey (© 12_Tribes), 5 dormouse (© Eric
Isselée), 5 toast (© travellight), 6 Aztec man (© Vladimir
Korostyshevskiy), 6 suitcase (© Stephen Coburn), 6
holiday photos (© maigi), 8 white statue (© Denis
Kornilov), 8 sports shirt (© Polryaz), 8 sports shorts (©
karam Miri), 10 hairdresser tools (© Rido), 10 Egyptian
woman (© Sergei Butorin), 11 (© Rachelle Burnside),
12 skyscrapers (© gary718), ferry (© Hannu Liivaar), 17
metal files (© optimarc), German money (© Patricia
Hofmeester), 17 old map (© Steven Wright), 17
compass (© Irina Tischenko), 18 (© Darren J. Bradley),
20 terracotta warriors (© bluefox), 21 soccer pitch (©
Peter Baxter), 21 terracotta warriors (© Txanbelin), 21
soccer (© Quang Ho), 21 golden goal (© diez artwork),
22 French flag (© c.), 22 Belgian flag (© ArtisticPhoto),
22 chips (© Africa Studio), 24 old paper scroll (© Irina
Tischenko), 24 egg (© Picsfive), 26 construction worker
(© Elena Elisseeva), 26 garden wheelbarrow with gold
(© Wire_man), 26 street paved with gold (© SueC), 28
Viking soldier (© Microprisma), 28 wooden house (©
bioraven), 28 sports car (© Michael Shake), 28 fire stripe
(© Jag_cz).

Cover photographs of Roman legionary soldier
(© Nejron Photo), brown bag (© Lim ChewHow),
and potato chips (© Africa Studio) reproduced with
permission of Shutterstock.

We would like to thank Diana Bentley and Marla Conn
for their invaluable help in the preparation of this book.

CONTENTS

Some words are shown in bold, **like this**. You can find out what they mean by looking in the glossary.

DID THE ANCIENT ROMANS EAT CHIPS?

That would be impossible! Potato chips are made from potatoes, which originally came from South America. The first potatoes only reached Europe in the 1500s— hundreds of years after the Romans had left.

EMPIRE CHIPS

SMELLY SANDALS FLAVOR

Did you know?

The Romans did like some very unusual snacks—including mice! The mice were coated in honey and sprinkled with poppy seeds.

DID THE AZTECS SEND POSTCARDS?

No, they did not! First of all, the **Aztecs** did not really go on vacations. But more importantly, the Aztecs could not really write. Instead, they used pictures to communicate with each other. For example, "night" would be shown with a black sky and a closed eye.

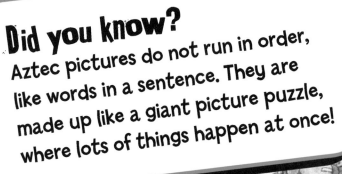

Did you know?

Aztec pictures do not run in order, like words in a sentence. They are made up like a giant picture puzzle, where lots of things happen at once!

WHAT TEAM UNIFORM DID ATHLETES WEAR AT THE ORIGINAL OLYMPICS?

Athletes at the ancient Olympics had no team uniform—because they did not wear any clothes at all! Women athletes were **banned**. To make sure this rule was never broken, the athletes had to compete naked.

Did you know?

Women were allowed to watch the Games—as long as they were **supervised** by a man.

This ancient Greek vase shows Olympic runners competing without any clothes.

SHOULD YOU SHAMPOO A PHARAOH?

Pharaohs did not need shampoo! Ancient Egyptians—especially important ones—usually shaved their heads. Then, they put on fancy wigs. The bigger and fancier your wig, the more important you were.

Did you know?

A golden razor found in Tutankhamun's **tomb** was still sharp enough to shave with, despite being over 3,000 years old!

WHICH CITY WAS BUILT FROM SHIPS?

In 1848, gold was discovered near San Francisco, California. People came from all over the world, hoping to become rich. Ships were abandoned in the harbor while the sailors ran off to look for gold! Local people used the ships to make all sorts of buildings.

Did you know?
Restaurants, stores, and even the local jail were built from old ships!

13

WHO WAS THE FIRST QUEEN TO USE A TOILET?

The first queen with a modern toilet was England's Elizabeth I. Her **godson**, John Harington, built it. It did not catch on. After Elizabeth's death, the royal toilet was torn down.

One would leave it a while...

Did you know?
In the olden days, most toilets were wooden benches with big holes in them. The waste dropped through the hole—usually into a river. Yuck!

HOW DID PRISONERS OF WAR PASS THE TIME?

During World War II (1939–1945), some British **prisoners of war** were sent board games by the people back home. But these were board games with a difference! Hidden inside were secret escape tools that they could use to escape from the German **POW camps** where they were being held!

I'm bored.

Game of Monopoly?

Items hidden in the Monopoly sets included metal files, money, a compass, and a map.

WHICH HORSE HAD A CITY NAMED AFTER HIM?

The horse was named Bucephalus. His owner was the Greek warrior-king Alexander the Great. Alexander spent his life conquering a huge kingdom. Bucephalus died in a battle far from home, in Pakistan. Alexander promptly named a new city after his beloved horse.

Welcome to **Horseville**

Did you know?
Alexander the Great was just 13 years old when he **tamed** Bucephalus.

DID ANCIENT CHINESE WARRIORS PLAY SOCCER?

Yes, they did. One of the earliest forms of soccer was an ancient Chinese military exercise. It was called *Tsu Chu*.

To score, players kicked a ball into a net. The warriors would have been good at taking **penalties**—the net opening was only 12 to 16 inches wide!

Nice, big goal...

Yes, this looks simple!

WHERE DID FRIES COME FROM?

Fries probably came from France—though some people claim it was actually Belgium. The first fries did not look like they do today. When rivers and lakes froze, people could not catch fish to eat. Instead, they cut potatoes into fish shapes and fried those.

Did you know?
American soldiers came to like fries—which they called "French fries"—during World War I (1914-1918).

DID PEOPLE IN ANCIENT CHINA WEAR NAIL POLISH ?

Yes, they did. The first nail coloring was probably used in China about 5,000 years ago.

Recipe for ancient Chinese nail color:
1. Mix beeswax, gum, coloring, and egg white
2. Paint on nails

Hey, presto—you have had an ancient Chinese makeover!

Did you know?
In ancient China, long
fingernails showed
you were important—
too important to
do physical work!

HAVE A CITY'S STREETS EVER BEEN PAVED WITH GOLD?

In the 1500s, stories told of an African city so rich that the streets were paved with gold. Its name was Timbuktu. Timbuktu's streets were never actually paved with gold—but it was very rich. Timbuktu was a center for the trade in salt and…gold.

Did you know?
The first **Westerner** to see the city of Timbuktu arrived in the 1820s.

DID THE VIKINGS USE GPS?

Vikings loved to travel. But they did not use GPS (global positioning systems) or satellites. Satellites were not invented for another 1,000 years.

But the Vikings did have a few navigation tricks:
1. Direction finders used the Sun's position to decide a course.
2. Sun boards used the Sun's shadow to figure out **latitude**.
3. Sunstones located the Sun when it could not be seen.

"You have reached your destination!"

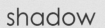

shadow pin

shadow

course
indicator

By lining up the Sun's shadow with the course indicator, the Vikings coud use sun boards to stay on the right course. But they were not very useful when it was cloudy!

GLOSSARY

Aztecs group of peope who lived in central Mexico hundreds of years ago

banned not allowed; against the rules

godson male person who an older person has promised to help and guide through life

latitude measure of how far north or south you are

penalty in soccer, a penalty is a kick at the goal taken from 12 yards (11 meters) away. Penalty kicks are defended only by the goalkeeper.

POW camp place where prisoners of war are held during a war

prisoner of war person captured by the enemy during war

supervise watch over to make sure things are done in the correct way

tamed no longer wild; made friendly to humans

tomb place where a dead body or bodies are kept

Westerner someone who lives in the West, particularly North America or Europe

FIND OUT MORE

Books

Bingham, Jane, Jane Shuter, Louise Spilsbury,
  and Richard Spilsbury. Time Travel Guides series.
  Chicago: Raintree, 2008.

Deary, Terry. *The Angry Aztecs and the Incredible
  Incas: Two Horrible Books in One*. New York:
  Scholastic, 2004.

Platt, Richard. Weird History series. Minnetonka, Minn.:
  Two-Can, 2007.

Web sites

Facthound offers a safe, fun way to find Internet sites
related to this book. All of the sites on Facthound
have been researched by our staff.

Here's all you do:
Visit *www.facthound.com*
Type in this code: 9781410951984

INDEX